Patchwork

CAROL WILSON-MACK

Patchwork

Conversations Between Generations

ReadersMagnet, LLC

"*The aged women likewise, that they be in behavior as becometh holiness, not false accusers, not given to much wine, teachers of good things; That they may teach the young women to be sober, to love their husbands, to love their children.*"

—Titus 2:3–4

This manuscript is dedicated to my fraternal grandmother, Anna Kirkland-Wilson, and maternal grandmother Carrie Nimmons-Dickerson.

These extremely strong women, both born in the 1800s had no choice but to be strong.

Grandma Carrie born to parents who longed for boys out of necessity often spoke about how her parents desired boys for they needed the boys to work the farms. It seemed that farming was what was done to feed families. Being the offsprings of slaves, farming was the only job they knew. Grandma Carrie's Mom and Dad bore girls so they raised their girls like boys. She fulfilled all the chores that a boy would do fishing, hunting, chopping cotton, chopping wood, picking cotton, and preparing cotton for the gin. (The gin was the machinery used to remove the seeds from the cotton, so that the cotton can be used for making clothing.) They were also required to assist with other chores, like cooking, cleaning, washing dishes, hauling wood, and packing the cotton in preparation for the gin. This involves assuring that no metal objects were lost in the cotton for that would damage and or hinder the gin's performance. Grandma Carrie even knew how to plow!

Ma Anna did not have to learn to plow, for she had many brothers, who did the plowing. Her job was to prepare their meals and deliver lunches and meals to the men in the fields.

Grandma Anna demonstrated the same inner strength; however in a more quiet gentler manner they both were insightful and kind. They shared the same mindset in that they both believed in being about their Father's business, which was teaching the younger generation, and they created the perfect platform to accomplish that goal.

This was my introduction to an organization that was founded, being organized and developed, as an ongoing group that was feeding God's first, and favored institution 'the family.' We must strive to keep our family strong and supported.

This group of women shared and supported each other in the face of whatever challenges, each may have been facing. They contributed greatly to the lives of each other as well as to the lives of those in each of the various families.

These strong courageous women were the first women whom I was privileged to have observed, as they gingerly helped the group of women that they were leading. They braced themselves to meet each challenge, and their focus was always on what was best for the families. They understood the fact, that our enemy Satan the devil would always attempt attacks on the family, simply because it was God's institution.

At the time, I was also being taught, though I was a youngster, I heard many of the stories, threaded many of the needles, bought and cleaned many of the eyeglasses, found scissors, cut thread, gathered straight pins, and searched for pin cushions. I remember thinking why can't they see these needle holes. I understand it now.

I sometimes felt the pain, and or understood bits and pieces of the emotions associated with some of the stories that they told, as much as I could understand. I responded to the needs of these Chief Executive Officers, as these nurturing creators rose to the level of obedience to the instructions from their heavenly Father. Patchwork reminds us of the multiple pieces of our life that we are required to juggle, as we interact with other lives and we do it continually and simultaneously.

As we put our pieces together, we attempt to maintain balance, as we proceed on our journey. We might remember also that while we piece our pieces together, there is a peacemaker, and he makes his peace available to all of us, provided we call upon him. Remember to call upon him as you juggle your pieces.

"Peace I leave with you, my peace I give unto you: not as the world giveth, give I unto you. Let not your heart be troubled, neither let it be afraid." John 14:27

Contents

Acknowledgments 11

Foreword.. 13

Chapter 1.. 15

Chapter 2: Mary 21

Chapter 3: Mary 29

Chapter 4: May Dell 33

Chapter 5: Sappy 39

Chapter 6: Magnolia 43

Chapter 7: Eleanor 48

Chapter 8 52

Chapter 9: Sappy 55

Chapter 10: Magnolia 60

Chapter 11: Eleanor 63

Chapter 12: May Dell 66

Chapter 13: Magnolia 70

Chapter 14: Instant Change 73
Chapter 15: Bits and Pieces.. 77
Chapter 16: Reflections by Trudy 79
Chapter 17: Trudy's Family Reunion...................................... 85
Chapter 18: There Is More 91

Acknowledgments

T O ALL THE GREAT LADIES and their families who had the mindset, were the co-creators, who stepped out in faith, following the directives of their loving creator. They started the Patchwork organization. My ancestors, I am grateful.

To Alma Wilson, my sister, I am grateful that you listened to my every word as the idea of Patchwork came to me your words were always encouraging.

To Stella Bobian, a great gospel singer, thank you for listening to my brainstorms as I pondered over ideas and past thoughts in the early stages of Patchwork. You were with me throughout the writing process, you sang "Burdens down Lord, Burdens down." As my character placed closure to her life's ordeal. I can still hear you singing. Great, great voice! Listen to her at CD baby/bobian.

Brother James H. Wilson I know I wore you out, asking "What do you think, how does this sound?"

Does it sound like something that someone would like to read? Forgive me, but you were always open and helpful and encouraging.

To Michael Baker, I could not have done this without you.

To Allen Craig Harris, one of the greatest actors that I know, busy, but you took the time to 'hear me' when I needed to be heard. Thank you.

My wonderful Uncle Freddie Dickerson who is the absolutely best Uncle that could be given to any family! I am so glad he is in mine! He is the absolute BEST!!!

Fritz Grant, at Readers Magnet this is the result of your heartfelt 'packaged' encouragement. Yes, it is always a package, and I like the Readers Magnet package that you guys represent. Each of you helped me along the way. I am grateful.

We really did develop a wonderful relationship. I thank you. Reader's Magnet staff must be the best in the nation!

Also helpful from ReadersMagnet, Mario Gonzaga, Ethan Dickinson, Sophia Stark, the wonderful the glorious Ms. Amie Bass, Jerry Randolph, Nikki Boltron and Ryza Rivers. I love you guys!

For all of you that I may not have mentioned by name, I am forever grateful for the role you played and I thank you.

I am grateful to God that I am in a country that provides opportunities and a positive encouraging group of people who steered me on. Thank you all!

—Carol Wilson-Mack

Foreword

PATCHWORK COVERS A PERIOD OF approximately forty plus years, positively contributing to the lives of the founders, as well as all those who were touched. These Precious people's efforts rippled over into an expanded time frame, thereby reaching generations of families.

It all began approximately 1939—through 1959—Anna's serving ways surfaced in her youth, however, her gift of giving continued as she eagerly shared her caring ways with friends and family. She believed that anyone and everyone who crossed our path was there for a specific reason and that God had allowed the paths to cross, and therefore she would gallantly stand up and be the representative for our Lord and Savior Jesus Christ. The kindness that she extended to her friends offered a much-needed strengthening, bonding and continuous bridge of support for those women and their families.

This group of women was an expertly organized group, despite the origin of its humble beginnings.

These Grandmothers were also daughters, sisters, wives, aunts, and teachers, and were both adept at organizing and leading. They both delved very naturally into their life's calling, it was not a struggle, it was a work that needed to be done, and they delighted in meeting the task.

It was a way to teach younger women how to deal with their challenges, how to choose prudent practices, and offered them the company, the support, the prayers and the wisdom of a solid support system.

The woman who was lovingly referred to as "Ma Anna" and "Ms. Carrie" supplied a safe place for the families to meet, work on their quilting, vent about their challenges, and work toward solutions. They were Founders if you will of this "Patchwork Organization."

The format of the gatherings changed over time; however, the concept of survival, sharing love, support learning through conversations between generations. Family unity and sharing were the underlying threads that assisted these families mostly in their lives.

The quilt was the physical focus, however, the patchwork was the other areas of the participant's lives that were "Patched together" as a result of these prayerful God-centered gatherings. The leadership provided by these great ladies touched the lives of many for generations! Please, continue reading.

—Carol Wilson-Mack

Chapter 1

"The name of the Lord is a strong tower: the righteous runneth into it and is safe"

—Prov. 18:10

THERE IS A WELL-DEFINED CHILL in the air this hazy September morning. Someone is walking briskly in the direction of Ma Anna and Papa John's home. A car was not always an affordable luxury during these days, walking to one's destination was a way of life for many families in South Carolina in 1939.

Who could that be? Ma Anna asked herself as she looked from the window. Their movement, their stride was with such determination that would suggest urgent, that something might be wrong. Whatever it is Ma Anna thought to herself it can be fixed with the Lord's help for he is able to see us through, no matter what it might be.

Ma Anna tried to think ahead for a possibility as to what the problem might be, as she thought about the usual things that the younger woman often spoke about and needed her assistance.

Anna Kirkland-Wilson stood 5ft. seven inches, a stately God-fearing, firm but a kind woman. Grandma Carrie her supporting consultant, was a mere 5 feet two inches. Grandma Carrie was also kind, firm, dedicated to helping, however, her kindness had to be earned.

Ma Anna relished on how she and Grandma Carrie could and would get things done as they put it, it was not they that were doing the 'doing' but it was always God. He was the lamp unto their feet. God guided their every step. Often the younger women would refer to these women as their "Beacons of Hope and light" They embodied the scripture that says "Where there is two or three gathered in my name there I am in their midst." They always gathered in his name.

Carrie Nimmons-Dickerson consulted with Ma Anna to help keep all plans on course. Their spiritual gifts were mercy for Anna and a firm teacher consultant for Carrie. Together these two gifts were working their ever-loving stitches into the lives that these women touched. They were God's daughters, being his hands and feet in the earth realm.

The approaching person is closer now, and Ma Anna recognizes her, its Mary Sultry.

"Hello Mary, how are you and your family?"

"Ma Anna we are all fine, thank you, and how are you and Papa John?

"Just fine, by the grace of God"

"I am concerned about Prince."

Mary, when a man is in the army, his life is not his own, his life is dedicated to defending the country.

Yes, mam, I know Mary responded, I know you speak the truth, however, I am concerned about Prince. I saw Prince not long ago, but just a day ago his uncle came to my house and asked me had I seen Prince. I found that unusual since our last time together, he planned to go to his family, or that's what I thought. As my place was his first stop when he was on leave.

"Don't fret my child," Ma Anna advised, as she consoled Mary. Let us pray that Prince is fine. We just have to trust in the Lord and take him at his word. We pray that everything is alright with

Prince, we must believe that, and if it's not, then we will be guided as to what we should do to fix it.

You can't do anything about something that you know absolutely nothing about. One must know enough about a particular situation before you can think of what to do about it, otherwise, you won't know what you are doing, just hold on to the promises of God, for he keeps his promises.

Mary Knew that what Ma Anna was saying made sense, however knowing, accepting and doing are two different things.

Mary felt a deep-rooted emotional pain as she agonized over memories of how she and Prince's recent time together was spent. She could never discuss that with Ma Anna, it was much too painful and personal. The thoughts kept running havoc in her head and were taking its toll on her life. The worst part was that she was unable to share them with anyone!

"Ma Anna you always find the words to make me feel somewhat better." Mary felt that when she attempted to engage in conversation with Ma Anna or with Grandma Carrie or with anyone, she struggled constantly because of the chitter-chatter in her head. These rapid thoughts bombarded her thinking. These wild thoughts have robbed her of her appetite and much too frequently steals her sleep as she lay restless in a bed that does not provide an outlet for anything, except for being a constant reminder of being present, bold and also being a blatant witness to the time when these sad memories occurred.

"Feel, better" Ma Anna's voice interrupted her thoughts. "God gives hope to us when we think that we have nothing to hold on to. Hope allows us an opportunity to move to our next step, but he tells us not to be anxious as we rest in his assurance that he will guide our steps. Are you receiving this Mary?"

"Yes, Mam I receive that in good faith thank you, however, I have another concern. The cold weather is fast approaching, it's early September and already it's a bit chilly. I need to make sure that I have enough quilts for my family." Ma Anna went to her storage closet and gave Mary a light bed covering. Ma Anna immediately knew what she would do to remedy this situation. Several of the other young women had approached her with the same concerns, bedding for their families. This was a challenge that needed her attention.

"Mary, listen to me," Ma Anna addressed Mary.

"Prepare yourself to come back to see me soon. I will arrange for a solution for this lack of quilts. We will summon the help of our friendly neighbors. You will gather every patch of cloth, if you like the patch, no you must love the patch! These quilts will be providing warm coverings for our love ones. This will not continue to be a problem for you, your children, or your children's children, for we will teach them to continue this tradition. God wants us to share information thereby each generation will be building, as we all strive to contribute to ourselves and mankind in whatever way we are gifted to contribute. We have an obligation and a responsibility to give it our very best.

In addition to the patches, gather thimbles threads, every color of thread that you have and bring them with you. We are going to do some patchwork for our families. I think we can get started right away. Please share with your husband; we want him to be in agreement with our plans.

Mary gathered the goodies that Ma Anna shared with her, and began her journey back to her home. She knew that Ma Anna would help her, for she had prayed and it was just as God promised his answers would be, over and beyond what we asked for. She was grateful. She walked hastily toward her home, which was not too far from Ma Anna, however in the South neighbors were neighborly and they shared in efforts to help each other Ma Anna was my nearest neighbor. I thank God for her kindness.

Ma Anna composed a letter. Which read:

September 19th, 1939

Dear Ladies,

There is an urgent need among us for bedding for our families. Winter is rapidly approaching; we will devise a plan that will correct this problem.

This is my plan that we come together to help each other by participating in a group effort, of making quilts for our families, for together we will speed up the process and increase the number of quilts that we can make.

Please, for all of you who can. Let's meet at my home on October 10th, 1939 at 10 am. We will begin some work for our families. I look forward to seeing you.

Please bring with you patches of cloths that you love, and all sewing notions (threads, needles, straight pins, scissors and please don't forget the needle threaders. I am looking forward to seeing you.

In the hopes of the master,
Anna Kirkland-Wilson

Anna shared with her husband John as to what her plans were.

"Why would you want to take on yet another thing to do," Papa John protested.

"Anna, don't you have enough to do? You wash and iron for the Stokes and Watson families, as well as your own family. You cook and clean your own place, as well as for everybody else. You plan butcher days during the winter months (butcher days is when a selected hog is killed and families are invited to assist, and they are rewarded with portions of the meat to help feed their families).

mind you Anna Wilson when you work yourself to death, I'll marry Isabella."

Ma Anna never failed to respond, "John Wilson, you will do no such thing, you won't get the chance for no one has ever died from hard work. Work is a gift from God, especially when that good deed is a kind gesture for someone else. John, I think what you need to do is get on your rusty knees and pray."

Papa John would explode in laughter. It was obvious that Ma Anna did what she decided to do with or without his approval. She addressed the letters and asked Papa John to deliver them to the ladies the next day.

John, I would like very much if you would deliver these letters to the ladies. Papa John always responded with a statement that suggested he did not want to do as she asked. "I am not your private mailman, suppose I don't want to deliver those old letters?"

"Oh, but you want to, that's right John you want to, I thought you knew that God had blessed me with my private mailman in John Wilson."

Papa John gathered the letters and promised her he would deliver them the next day, providing Moses his mule will cooperate. Oh, Moses will be willing that's what he does take messages to God's people, I just have to get you as on board as Moses.

"Lord I thank you for John Wilson, and thanks to you John Wilson for all that you do!

Chapter 2

MARY

"And my God shall supply all your needs according to his riches in glory by Christ Jesus."

—Philippians 4:19

T HE WOMEN CAME TOGETHER TWO weeks later as planned. They bought bundles of patches as well as other notions. They gathered around as they spread the patches so that Mary might select the patches that she desired for her quilt. Everyone looked on and assisted as needed as Mary joyfully chooses the patches that she liked and then the sewing began! Each lady sewed together individual patches which would then be coordinated with the larger whole.

The women looked forward to coming together. They knew that it was their duty to honor and care for their families. It was a God-given assignment.

They also anticipated that they would be looked upon and scrutinized for meeting and or coming together. The white people would become suspicious when any group of more than two of us come together, for whatever reason. They cannot accept the idea that we too have business ideas or things that we choose to do independent of any directives and or input from them.

They cannot embrace the fact that we might be able to do anything without input from them. They believe that we are not normal level headed human beings, even though we offered supportive labor, nurturing to their families, cook their meals, breastfed their children, wash their clothes, and countless other chores.

Just as expected, like clockwork a car pulled up. It was Mr. H. Stokes one of the men that Ma Anna did laundry for.

"Is everything alright?" Mr. stokes asked.

"Just a bunch of gossiping women coming together to gossip some more" Ma Anna responded.

"He knows Ma Anna is ok he is just being nosey!" Mary said. Sappy joined her.

"Of course he's nosey and nothing gets them more nervous, then when they see more than two of us coming together."

"I understand why!" Eleanor chimed in.

"When people have done as many hateful acts, so many evil deeds and downright wrong, and never have been held accountable, they must embody fear, for they may never know when any one of us might reach our breaking point and suddenly rise against them. We all know that fear is not of God. We know that he has not given us a spirit of fear. However, everybody has a breaking point. How much can we take?"

"Apparently we can take a lot for God knows a lot has been dished out to us and it is definitely by the grace of God that we are still here." Ma Anna said.

"You said a mouthful, Ma Anna" Sappy said.

How is it, that we call them people? Who told us they were people? We call them people, and they call us animals.

Sappy went on to ask the question that she described as a burning question. That is if it was the other way around would they still be here?

I don't believe it could be the other way around, for we don't have the heart to be so cold so heartless and downright cruel. We could never treat them as they have treated us.

Some of us are learning how to be mean, learning to mimic the hateful behaviors. Being mean is not a natural trait for us. That may be one of the main reasons that we are so easily taken advantage of, because we feel, we are compassionate.

All my life I have been thinking of things that I might do to get out of the rut, to improve things for myself my family and my people and I have not been successful to this day. I am seemingly running out of things to do.

"But they are not too fearful, they don't worry about us, we're women. We are no threat to them. It's a different story when the men come together that's when they show concern, to the point they will do whatever it takes to break up what they perceive as a threat to them.

"We all have husbands or boyfriends we can get our men together." Mary stated.

"We can?" Ma Anna asked with a sly grin on her face. The ladies chuckled, for they all knew Papa John. "My husband, the one you call Papa John, getting him to do something is like planning a trip to the dentist."

John Wilson will give you a song and a dance.

Well, Eleanor began, at least you get a song and a dance, I get a, a, she could not find the words to accurately describe her husband. The women laughed.

Now, now ladies Ma Anna interrupted. Remember the reason we have come together. Let us continue in love as we prepare our quilts. We want always to share a spirit of love and caring. I understand that these feelings and discussions will surface from time to time. Many times we may be compelled to address some of them however I would like us to move forward in love and establishment of the rules that will govern this group.

Deep in her heart, she knew exactly what the women were expressing. She shared their feelings and concerns. She knew that she had to steer them clear of this kind of thinking for it could not be solved here and it would add a heavy laborious component to their gatherings. It would take us out of the task at hand which was making coverings that are infused with love for our loved ones and we did not need to ever speak of those outlandish inequalities that have ravished our world.

Will we ever learn and accept the fact, that God put us in this world together, and there is certainly enough room for all of us and he specifically asked us to "Love one another." He did not say love those with white skin only.

She adjusted her position in her chair as any chief executive officer might do and looked around the room, rather pleased with the number in attendance, and very happy that she gets to offer her service in this way. Whatever we do, we are to do it as unto the Lord. She is looking forward to the fruits that will unfold from this group. She felt that she was called by the almighty to fulfill this task, which will benefit all of our families.

"Ladies, the few rules that we will follow, please feel free to add, discuss or bring up anything that you feel should be added and is good for all of us. Our gatherings will be scheduled every two weeks and or more frequent if the need becomes more urgent. There are five families represented here. God is our leader we will move forward according to God's direction, and this group of women will work together to bring our projects to fruition. We will be working for our families, and we pray that many will reap the benefits of our efforts for generations to come."

Ma Anna paused and waited for the women to speak, no one had anything to add she immediately went into prayer.

"Oh heavenly Father, your daughters sit before you in support of our families. Help us to be in harmony one with the other. Help us to always escape the snares of the enemy and Father keep us safe. We know that you are in our midst. Bless each and every one of us, and meet us at our point of need. Bless our projects as we move forward in the name of your son Jesus Christ we ask this. Thank you. Amen."

She then greeted each of the women warmly and reaching out to each one individually letting them know the importance of the contributions that each one of them was contributing.

Mary Sultry, Sappy Jordan, Magnolia Wilkes, Eleanor Watts, and May Dell Grant. I thank you all for taking part in this project. We will accomplish great things. First, let us establish our rules to which we all must abide. Yes, we will report every two weeks as our lives allow. We will remember each other in prayer and we will not share our discussions with others outside of this circle. They may not wish us the best. We must not allow any negativity to enter and penetrate our purpose. We will promote love, family, connection, and unity. We will change the subject if needed if a person who is not of the circle should appear, and seem to represent something negative. We will feel it for we have a spirit that will help us discern a person and or a situation. These are our basic rules.

Everyone here will be sewing for Mary. We will follow her selections, and be a loving supporter in the making of her bed covering for her family. Our conversations then will be centered on Mary and the kind of challenges that she and her family may be facing. In other words, our focus will be for the family whose quilt we are sewing.

Mary is the inspiration for the forming of this group so maybe she has some concerns that she would like to share that we may assist her in that way as well. We must respect the privacy of each other and vow and agree not to discuss the personal challenges that each of us may face outside of this group. This is very important.

If there are any other women whose need, and desire is to join us, please invite her, if you feel that she will adhere to our rules and regulations, and will participate, please invite her. The invited woman's husband must be in agreement with her participation with this group. We don't need any Thomasinas. We all understand who Thomasinas might be right? In the event that you are not aware of whom Thomasinas might be, they are the sisters to Uncle Toms. Everyone understood.

Mary, will you share your concerns?

"Thank you for helping me. I am truly grateful." The women are sewing as Mary begins to share.

"A few weeks ago, I was at home it was late evening, and my seven-year-old niece Trudy whom I care for, after a fatal accident, and she lost both of her parents. Trudy begged me to allow her to play outside later than usual. She loves to play with lightning bugs. Trudy told me that Prince, the love of my life, had come by and that she played hopscotch and he helped her catch lightning bugs.

I saw Prince that same evening as he came over to see me in my wing of our home. You all know how large that old house is. Most of you know Prince; however, for those of you who don't know him, I will share a little about him.

Prince is a man who does not look for trouble however he does not back down from trouble if trouble comes his way. Prince is a serious man yet he can be loving and playful with those he loves. He is firm but kind. He stands six feet three inches tall, and has a perfectly chocolate complexion. He is handsome, well-loved and has a perfect physique. A man of a few words, but when he spoke people knew he had something to say. Sometimes his presence seemed to antagonize some people. His intensity was piercing. His presence could not be denied. His quiet intense demeanor was difficult for some to endure.

Last week Prince's uncle came to see me and wanted to know if I had seen Prince. The moment he asked me, I feared that something had happened to him. I explained to his uncle that I did not expect to see Prince anymore, as we experienced a big disagreement when we were together, and decided to walk away from each other despite the fact that we loved each other."

What do you mean you walked away from each other, Ma Anna wanted to know. Well, I did not plan to see him anymore. Sometimes we have to make choices, that we may not like, but we do it because it is what we think is best for each of us at the time.

The women were in shock. Those who knew Mary and Prince all expected that Mary and Prince would be married someday.

"The night Prince came to see me," Mary continued "He was on leave from the military. You know Trudy and I cried three days or more when he was drafted to the army. He was such a big part of both of our lives. We knew that we would not be the same. We both were in agony over his leaving for his military deploy.

The uncle told me that the family had recently received a letter saying that Prince was away without official leave. His uncle said he was due home last month but he did not come. The family did not hear from him. Last month was about the time Prince came to see me. It is not like Prince to not go to see his family. I was surprised for when he left me I thought he was going to his family."

"Oh my lord," Ma Anna commented as the group continued sewing furiously, while listening to Mary's story.

"So why do you think something happened to him?" As the others looked on, they too had the very same question in their eyes.

"Because of the nature of our disagreement," Mary replied.

Ma Anna assured Mary that disagreements can be fixed.

"This one can't be fixed, Ma Anna," she said as she struggled to hide the tears that slowly dripped from her eyes, after which she started to cry uncontrollably. The women consoled her as best they could. They each offered words of comfort to Mary and assured her that they would keep her in prayer. The group closed with prayer and felt that if nothing else Mary was able to vent, and know that she was among people who cared about her and offered her their sincere support. They advised her not to worry and encouraged her to speak about it further when she felt ready to continue sharing. She was also reminded that the sooner she decided to speak about it, the sooner she would begin to heal the scars that the damage may have caused.

Everyone is in anticipation of seeing the completion of Mary's quilt as they each departed for the day.

Chapter 3

MARY

Prince's uncle headed back and informed his family of the information that Mary had shared with him. Yes, she did see Prince about a month ago. It seems the family for whatever reason did not see him. The family then filed a missing person's report, and began waiting and hoping for the best.

Approximately one month after the police report was filed; an object was spotted by fisherman, in the Santee River. The object was hauled from the river, and it turned out to be a defaced body. It was discovered just outside of the district of Prince's home town. This then placed the immediate investigation under the jurisdiction of the next county. The body was mangled with rope and was not recognizable.

Upon further investigation, it was learned later, that the body was tied to an old car motor, in an effort to hold it down into the depths of the Santee River.

The body emerged and made itself visible. It was identified and confirmed to be that of Prince Moss. Who had been reported missing the last month.

Prince majestically displayed his lofty presence in death as he so often did in life. His quiet presence was always known.

There was an investigation, but soon it ended and was filed as an unsolved mystery.

The family was devastated! Prince came home on leave from the army to visit with his family and ends up dead, how did this happen? He was well-liked, and was the perfect gentleman so who wanted Prince dead?

How does a man go to the United States Army to defend his country and come home to visit with his family and is never to be seen again? One would think the likelihood of being killed in the army is higher than in civilian life and or is it?

Mary and Trudy were in shocking disbelief when they got the news! Mary continued attending the quilting sessions, but she was not herself. Mary became distant from the group long before she heard of Prince's death. However, immediately afterwards, she was more distant. She marched into our sessions, walked over to her chair, flopped her body into the chair, she continues to sew, but no words passed between her lips, except good morning, thank you and good night.

She was depressed and seemed not able to embrace her surroundings. She was not able to lift herself out of this oblivion.

As a support group, we prayed and cried with her. We wiped her tears. We rocked her. We sang with her. We engaged in helping her and his family with funeral plans. Both families were greatly grieved. It seemed her life was buried with Prince's remains.

She was on the other side of sad. Her pain was deep. She built a wall that we could not penetrate. Everyone tried; she would not let us in. She became so closed, even the word of God began to bounce off of her. We planned visiting days with her when we were not scheduled for our sewing sessions, no progress. She lost an excessive amount of weight. Food was not a part of her daily routine. We were deeply concerned about her well-being. She was unable to get past Prince's death. We even lost contact with her niece Trudy.

We asked God to bring Mary back to us but deep down we knew that she had to want to come back. We believed that when you pray for someone it is important that they be in agreement with the prayer that you pray. Mary was not in agreement with our prayers. That is why when you agree to pray for someone, you might ask the person what should I ask God for on your behalf? Then the two of you will be joining in faith when you approach the Father, and you know what he said when two or three is joined in my name, there I am in the midst. Physical joining together is good; however spiritual joining is also needed. Our faith is then joined thereby doubling our effort of faith to the Father.

One of us may not have enough faith to accomplish the deliverance of our request, however, if we join forces, then our faith is enhanced by the addition of the other person's faith and surely God is there because he said he would be. We must take him at his word. If we pray for each other as he asked us to do, you are doing your part. If you do your part, then God will surely do his part, rest assured.

We should never depend solely on another to pray for us. What if they forget? What if they fall asleep? It is important to pray for yourself. This is one thing you might say 'If I want it done I better do it myself!' If they also prayed, then that's a bonus.

You talk to God; he does not ask us for perfection, he wants us to remember him. Do not forget me was his request to the Israelites of the Old Testament and it is his request to us today, do not forget me. He wants us to acknowledge our dependence on him, and call upon him for our every need. He is waiting to fulfill his promises to those who believe. Let us be like the man in Mark 9:24, "I believe

Lord help thou my unbelief. And say Lord I believe, help thou my unbelief."

The next quilt is progressing at rapid speed, we are grateful.

Chapter 4

MAY DELL

THE GATHERING CONVENES AT ITS usual time; however, one member is absent, Mary. No one has heard from her. Several attempts were made to her home, without success. The group continued to pray for her, that she may come into agreement with what God's plan for her life; for we know for sure that God does not want her to go on as she is going.

The group's prayer was that she becomes aware of the provisions that God has for her, and that she has the willingness and courage to recognize and follow his lead. God will provide her with the strength; she must be faithful enough to step into all that he has provided. And God will strengthen her as she moves forward with her life.

Mary is absent, so May Dell then decided that she will share what has been a challenge for her and her family.

"I feel that you all know my story. May Dell began. You all know my family. You also know that my daughter Maysee is my 'different child.' She is my different child in every way. I cannot deny that but this will be the first time in my life that I am able to talk about it. I can no longer deal silently with how she was conceived.

It breaks my heart every day of my life. In my household, we walk around and talk around as if everything is alright. I cannot imagine what my child must be going through at school. She is an extremely quiet child, withdrawn and her entire persona is sadness. I don't know what I can or cannot say, or what I should or should not do, when, and if she questions me, as to why she looks so different from her sisters and brothers. I know even less to say when I look into my husband's eyes but on this unspoken topic both races are in generational denial, as we are, however clearly for different reasons.

It is said that slavery has been long over, however in the mind of some of these white men, they believe that they still owe us, that we are just property that they can use at will and in whenever and whatever capacity that serves them. He is at liberty to have sex with the wife of one of his sharecroppers, with no respect for the colored union.

I could never imagine how one could feel so privileged to that extent. Even if one feels privileged, the next human being is also privileged, and it is not dependent upon whether you believe it. It is so because it is so. The creator has placed us here so, therefore, everybody that's here is supposed to be here.

The stranger part of the matter is that many of the white wives know about these situations and they tolerate it, why? Is it out of fear or do they pretend that they don't know. Am I expecting too much, and or what am I expecting the wife to do? She too is in a situation that is, is, oh I can't explain it!

Often the wife's behavior changes toward the woman whom her husband is raping at will. She seems to blame the woman for her husband's wrong behavior. She is angry with her husband, and she spits that anger toward the woman, me and too many others. It is an ugly and absolutely impossible situation. They believe that the word married applies only to them. They are disrespecting their union! You would think that they would understand that. I gather that understanding does not always supply accurate behavior.

They feel that we are not human, that we are animals. Well, are they comfortable having sex with animals? I gather he feels that he does whatever he wants to do whenever he wants. I feel that if I don't get some kind of release from these thoughts, I will just burst wide open. My Grandma shared a story with me that is so unbelievable. I had never heard this one, and I have heard many. The story is that sometimes one of the slaves was chosen to lie at the foot of the bed, beneath the covers, for the purpose of supplying heat to the feet of the Caucasian Massa. Can you believe that one? Three of the women had not heard that one either. Shocking!

My Maysee's eyes are the saddest eyes that I have ever seen. There is absolutely nothing I can do to make her feel better. I can't protect her from the daily onslaught of pain that is slurred toward her in the form of dirty words, horrible whispers, silly and hurtful pranks that she gets from cruel children, etc. yet we lie to ourselves chanting "Sticks and stones may break my bones but words will never hurt me." Words can be and often is very hurtful and contribute oftentimes to long term emotional scarring.

I feel that I am shouldering my pain that is so heavy, that I don't have enough strength to help my child with her pain load or the others in my household yet it is my responsibility. Neither I or my child is responsible for the pain we must bear, we cannot escape it. It is in every part of our very being.

If only she had not been conceived May Dell cried out in agony. Then we would not have to walk around and talk around as we do. Yet, had she not been conceived, the act continues for all that are victims of this unequal selfish act!

I have a living witness that walks around, and I am her mother. I am required to love her, yet we walk around loving each other none the less, but we are not able to show it in loving open ways, for the shame of the situation is so intense and heavy we just don't know what to do, what to say and or sometimes where to even look! My Maysee's gaze is filled with questions and my glance is a choice as to not wanting to remember and or, to acknowledge or even to define the circumstance and or circumstances. We avoid, we feel shame, and we feel completely helpless why do we feel so helpless? Sometimes we don't feel at all. Is it because we have begun to believe what they are saying about us? They don't even believe it. They want to justify how they treat us, but they are in generational denial. We have been for generations! We have lived with the conflict of this battle in our minds. I am sure in our minds we have often thought who am I? Only to try and remember, our cultural beauty, our homeland and then become so bombarded with the cruelty that is, so harsh, until we are forced to choose between culture and survival. These critical choices have to be made often very quickly, while all at the same time we are trying to adjust to a strange land, and a strange group who calls themselves people, but they behave like animals. They call us animals, while we treat them with as much dignity and respect that we can muster, all while our priority and craving would have to be survival.

This state of affairs will continue, unless we share information with each generation and build, we must hold on to our culture, to our way of life. We must build from generation to generation.

Ladies, I tell you that some days my Maysee staggers in from school, I surmise that the children have been so mean, saying things to her that she does not understand, and when she gets home things that she fears to ask about because she does not know how or what to ask. I believe that she feels that she does not fit in at school, and neither does she fit in at home, where then can she go? That has got to be an awful feeling.

Yes she is the offspring of a "Massa" rape. Yes, he raped the wives of his sharecroppers! Oh my God, that is the first time I have ever said that aloud. He still owns us. He raped me over and over and I have living proof in Maysee. I know that I am not the only one that this is happening to. I can look at the other women. There is a look that we exchange, and somehow we know, but we never talk about it.

But for me, my proof is one of my children. She is ever-present, and she walks around on display for everyone to see. I don't blame the child, God knows I don't, she is the innocent one and a participant by default. How do I love this child unconditionally when each time I see her I am reminded of those encounters that are so unbalanced, so discolored, so physical and so whatever else? No matter how hard you try she becomes that living reminder.

The only thing you can do is to acknowledge that you love her, but in a different way from the way you love the other children. The way she was conceived is not in harmony with God's plan. That "Massa" was not your meet, as a couple is supposed to come together as God designed the union. Gen. 2:18 states: "And the Lord God said, it is not good that man should be alone: I will make him a help meet for him."

By the grace of God, you love her as best as you can, in every way that you can, as much as you can and be at peace with oneself. You might ask God to strengthen you for it is true that we can do all things through Christ who strengthens us. This is truly an example of one of the most difficult of the test!

I grieve for my child. It seems that there is no relief and or escape from the sadness that envelopes our lives.

The next quilt has just begun. Ma Anna began a prayer:

"Oh, heavenly Father we pray for May Dell and her family. We ask a special prayer for Maysee. We know that our children are gifts from you, help this mother to focus on the gift giver and thank him for the gift that he entrusted to her care, despite the circumstances. Father, we know it is hard; however, it helps us to remember to rely upon you, for we cannot do this in our own strength. We thank you for that realization. Keep her focused on Jesus. Father we ask you to bless every person who lies beneath the coverings that you have given us the ability to create, may their lives be filled with your love and your will, we thank you for your grace in Jesus' name. Amen."

Chapter 5

SAPPY

EVERYONE, I HAVE A GRAVE concern for my granddaughter. My concern may sound minor to you all; comparatively, it may be considered minor, however, it is my concern.

An entire family is dependent upon this child to be the first to attend college in this family. I am so worried now that her mind has shifted. She is our only hope for this generation, it's her choices that will inspire the next generation, and now she does not even talk about school and schoolwork, she is running to the radio when school is out. to listen to music.

I told you that she was a good student; however, as of late I am not so sure, for now, she seems to daydream a lot. She sits by the radio waiting to hear some man sing a song on the radio. She does not even know the man's name and neither does she know the name of the song that he is supposed to be singing, now how do you like that ladies? A good student and her entire family is counting on her to be the first in our family to attend college, and now she has developed a habit of just sitting by the radio waiting for a man to sing a song.

Now listen, don't you worry yourself, her wait won't be too long for there are male singers singing on the radio all the time. She will soon hear him, and everything will be back to normal.

Oh Ma Anna it's not just any male singer it's a special one, but she does not know his name, and neither does she know the name of the song he is singing.

She will find her way. She likes school and she loves learning. The man on the radio will not stop her. Give her a chance. Give her the benefit of the doubt. It's ok that she likes to listen to the man on the radio.

She is not just listening to the radio for any singer it is a special singer whose name she does not know and whose song she cannot say its name.

Well, let her hear the man. The man cannot harm her from the radio. Sappy, Sappy Ma Anna repeated her name. "Sappy, Sappy. You are allowing your thinking to get away from you. We will be praying for you and your family. So rest assured that your granddaughter will be ok, she will surely find her way."

The youngsters get excited over singers. But you know your grandchild she will not go astray remember the scripture that reads bring up a child in the way he should go, and when he is old he will not stray?

If you say so Sappy responded, "I say so," Ma Anna answered her.

She will soon be out of high school and you will soon celebrate the first member of your family to attend college. So look forward to that day this is simply a minor bump in the road she will get back on track.

Maybe you are right Ma Anna Sappy said, Her Dad always told her that school was the answer and she definitely believes him.

That is a good thing they all said in unison, as the sewing continues.

"How is your Father?" Ma Anna asked Sappy.

"He is fine he is looking forward to hearing about the first in the family to attend college. I would not dare tell him that his prospect for college is not speaking about college, but have replaced college thoughts with running to the radio, it may frighten him.

This family makes many sacrifices for her. Many of us do without things that she can have adequate school supplies, nice clothes so she can study and begin to make a positive change for this family. Money for her books and these are big sacrifices for a family that is already strained and not having enough.

This is an effort to contribute to the next generation; she cannot be allowed to spoil our family plans and sacrifices. Well Papa went as far as he could during his time. He did not have the freedom of attending school throughout the school year. They had to come out of school to maintain the farm. In his day, school started in August. He went to school the first day to register, and then he was kept out of school until after Christmas! They were expected to maintain their grades and be ready to move on to the next grade level.

Believe it or not, he is planning a school reunion with his school and the few classmates that he has left.

He now lives in that long term care facility. He likes it there. He thinks that he is the apple of the nurse's eyes. He does not want to be a burden on the family, though we never saw him as a burden; however, we are free from struggling to find someone to be with him when we go to work.

"God bless him" Ma Anna continued. When one is healthy one is truly blessed. We support and pray for your family.

The women are now preparing to leave, sharing their wishes for continued prayer. They each depart in peace with additional assurance of peace and support.

Chapter 6

MAGNOLIA

"LADIES!" MAGNOLIA BEGAN. "I AM not as sure as to how to start saying what I have to say, all I know is that I have something to say, for I have been carrying this load for far too long, I am indeed heavy laden."

Ma Anna said, remember God teaches us to come to him, all of us who are heavy laden, he invites us to come to him and he will give us rest. Matthew 11:28–30

Take your time the ladies told her we can wait until you are ready and able to share. I believe I'm ready. Magnolia began. So you ladies remember my Grandma Cecelia?

Oh yes, Ma Anna responded. I remember her very well, a grand lady she was.

She may have been grand as you say I wish I could remember her grandeur as you say, however, what I remember about her as being a very strict mean lady, Sappy said. "Oh yes, she tore up my behind too many times with one of those great big old switches.

She would beat anybody's child. She believed that children should be seen but never heard. And God forbid if you should say something when a so-called grown person is talking. She believed that it does take a village to raise a child and anybody in that village could beat the child, but she was entitled to first beating rites. She was 'The beater' of the neighborhood. I believe something is wrong with that thinking. You have a reputation for beating people, especially little children. I believe in discipline, but is beating the only way?

It was all she knew, she learned it from well, I don't need to say it, you know.

We miss Ms. Cecelia, I think she has been dead for about four years now. I don't miss those beatings that she gave out for the least little thing a child did. Many of the children were so afraid of her that they would hold their breath when they passed by her house or even if they saw her. They thought she would whip them for breathing. One little girl passed out, I think she held her breath too long.

Ladies, Ma Anna began, we never know what one may have had to do, what one may have had to witness, to observe that may have caused her to be so strict she may have witnessed many beatings, and or hangings even as a girl. Those kinds of things harden people's hearts. All the children thought that she was just a mean old lady.

Ma Anna attempted to try and make sense so that the ladies might understand. You see when a group has been so oppressed they begin to behave like the oppressor. They begin believing that this is the way one has to behave. They copy the awful beatings from their Massa and they pass it down to their generations. We must teach love and tolerance of each other, and the color of skin does not matter! When will we get that?

When we are born into a household, we only know that household. Children think that every household is like their home. Until they grow older and discover that each dwelling is different. This is not who we are and what we do. We must choose to teach love instead of hate, regardless of the injustices in the world.

I heard a spiritual teacher who said he could not speak for every one of us, but he stated that he did not believe that we teach our children to hate. He once experienced seeing some very young white children who was seeing a Negro man for the first time, and in his excitement he shouted "look Daddy, a chocolate man!" The father replied, "That's not a chocolate man! That's a nigga!" The intensity of his delivery, the tone of his words made the child feel that "nigga" is not something good.

So now that child will go forward in life hearing and maybe using that obnoxious word in reference to Negro people.

We may be losing our loving culture, our loving nature's and took on this hateful, fearful nature of this "Massa" in an effort to survive. Magnolia let us get back to your story.

This is about Louise, my oldest sister and Will, my youngest brother. Shortly before Grandma Cecelia died.

Will told me something years ago, and I put it out of my mind, I never told anyone for he made me promise not to tell anyone. He was so afraid of Louise and because he was just seven years old, I wanted to keep my promise I can still hear him saying "You Promise?" But that promise has caused me to question my decision, especially when I hear him speak with that whisper. There was a time when he could not or did not speak at all, and then when he did speak it was with that whisper. Upon examination, the Doctors could not find any physical reason for him not to speak. On this particular day, Grandma Cecelia had whipped Louise for something that she had done, for she was extremely mischievous. Grandma beat her unmercifully after sending her to bring her the switch that she whipped her with. I felt sorry for her that day despite the numerous pranks she played on me. Louise chose a small switch, Grandma marched her right back to the tree and this time Grandma chooses a much bigger switch and she beat her all around the house. Louise was so mad and Will heard her say she was going to fix Grandma. Will also heard her say she refused to take anymore beatings from Grandma. She threatened Will by telling him if he told anybody she would fix him, just as she fixed Grandma.

Grandma loved grape Kool-Aid. Louise sometimes helped with preparing the family meals and making the Kool-Aid was often something that she did. It was long after the beating Louise asked grandma if she wanted some Kool-Aid. After drinking the Kool-Aid Grand Ma became very ill. She never recovered and she died shortly afterward. After Grandma's death, Will stopped speaking. He could not, or would not speak. Will told me that Louise told him that she put rat poison in Grandma's Kool-Aid and if he tells anyone she would fix him just like she fixed grandma.

It was as if he stopped speaking, to assure that he would not tell anyone of the threats that Louise made toward him. When he did speak it was in a strange whisper. I did not think of this for many years until I heard about the death of Louise's husband.

It was said that Louise was very confrontational. Everyone who had ever been in her company in any social gathering, either witness this or was told about it by someone's gossip. She would ignite disagreements between people and promoted fights.

She was at a social gathering once and there were nice bottles of wine leftover on the tables. Some bottles were not consumed during the event. She began gathering bottles, but just as her hand landed on the would-be her second bottle, a gentleman's hand landed at the same time. It was the fifth size bottle.

"If you don't remove your hand," Louise bellowed "I will burst the one that I have over your head." She said to the man. The man did not move his hand. The gentleman's wife said, "Sweetheart I think we can do without that bottle of wine if she need it let her have it."

"I don't need it," Louise said, "but he is not going to have it!"

"Please," the wife pleaded with her husband, "just walk away." He did. Louise was an intimidating person. She was also a very tall, large woman, and her voice was loud and boisterous.

"My Lord!" Ma Anna said "I regret that you were laden with that for such a long time. God help you. Do you really think that Louise was capable of doing something so outrageous?"

Yes, I do, as I think back and think of the many hateful pranks that she pulled. She once buried Will at the beach. With only his head above the surface. She tricked him, telling him she would allow him to bury her, it started out as fun, but she left him for a long while, the poor thing almost cried his eyeballs out. She left him, but my other brother rescued him for he knew Louise's behaviors.

I regret that Will and others endured such mean tricks from Louise. God knows we can play together and be kind to our family and friends. Your family is not the only family that has secrets, and secrets I believe are rooted in shame and fear.

Let us conclude for today and let us continue our prayers for each other.

"Lord help your children. We cannot change or undo the past, but we can live a blessed life and keep on leaning on you to guide us through this life and give us the ability to move forward and give us your healing and peace to the mind of Magnolia. We know that you can make all things work together for our good, even when the enemy means it for bad. Thank you, Father, for this assurance, in the blessed name of Jesus. Amen."

Chapter 7

ELEANOR

❧

Eleanor (left)

M A ANNA OPENED THE GATHERING by announcing that Eleanor will be speaking today. Her family challenges involved her sisters.

Eleanor begins. My father was a colored man; my two sister's father was a Native American. The sisters were extremely close to each other, and their closeness made Eleanor feel excluded. They accepted me as their sister; however, they clung so close to each other and there was not anything for me to feel but left out. Our Mom was also guilty though not with conscious intent, however, guilty nonetheless. I felt pain from the behavior of my Mom and sisters in a deep and hurtful way.

My sisters Jeanette and Andrea are not twins, however, they behave like twins. Jeanette had a boyfriend who adored her. He was a kind, handsome, and loving man and he shared his caring nature with those in whom he came in contact. Everybody loved him. He recognized the distance that the sisters created toward Eleanor, and without realizing it, he filled that void with his kindness and his acceptance of her. It did not matter to him that her Dad was not the same Dad as Jeanette and Andrea, and certainly not the fact that he was colored. He lightened the sullen pain that Eleanor experienced.

I always felt happy when George came to visit Jeanette; he bought joy into our home. I would like you all to join me in prayer, as I pray right now for my sisters. They all stopped sewing momentarily as Eleanor prayed.

"Heavenly Father these ladies join me and I come humbly before you requesting help for Jeanette and Andre. Lord, help Jeanette to see that George really loves her, and help her to rid herself of her jealous nature. Help her to know that the quality that she loves in George is also seen by others, and they love him also. Lord help them to have a more peaceful life. Help her to accept his love for what it is, and rid herself of her jealousy when he interacts with others. Help us to love and support each other, in Jesus' name Amen.

I have to commend you for praying for your sisters. Ma Anna said, you recognize jealousy for the evil that it is, yes it brings disharmony into our lives, that's why God says love one another.

When one recognizes jealousy within themselves, it would be to one's best interest to do whatever it takes, to learn how not to serve jealousy. Each of us has been created and is placed on this earth, each of our spiritual gifts may be different, and however, we are here to serve each other, not to envy and or be jealous. We serve him our master by serving each other, no matter how hard that may be at the time.

Oh yes, Sappy added jealousy is a pickle. It will and can keep you bitter if you let it. We need help from God to rid ourselves of something as caustic as jealousy. The vessel that holds jealousy is the one that is damaged most by its galling concentration.

Jeanette and Andrea loved to socialize. Parties were a big part of their lives. Jeanette's jealousy prevented her sometimes from truly enjoying the social gatherings. Jeanette became so upset with George if he talked to anyone, including me. All the women loved to talk to George and many of them flirted openly with George simply to annoy Jeanette. He and I got along fine because I understood this part of him. He was a free spirit, and he was at ease mingling with people. I could not understand why Jeanette had such difficulty with accepting the nature of the man she loved. Everyone knew George loved Jeanette, however, Jeanette was never satisfied. Maybe she did not know what would satisfy her longing, or maybe she did not know what she was longing for. Despite the attention that George showed her, it was never enough.

During one of the social gatherings, which was mostly held in some one's home, a woman had drank too much, and began to flirt openly with George. Jeanette became so enraged with George, she pulled a knife on him as she thought George was encouraging the woman in her pursuit for his attention; however, he was being the gentleman that he was making sure that the woman was not injured as he assisted her from her fallen position. It is a grim memory of that fatal night. The police was summoned.

I saw George slump over, I was so afraid. We all were. Our fun night had a sudden fatal twist. There was blood everywhere. George was breathing but each breath became more labored than the one before. The police arrived. They began their questioning, "What happened here?" Who lives here? What relationship are you to the injured, etc. it was question after question.

George feebly gestured for the police's attention as he lay in a pool of blood and could barely speak. The officer kneeled and lowered his head to attempt to hear what George was trying to say, everyone was looking on and the officer repeated George's statement in the form of a question, "It was an accident?" as the officer eyes scanned the crowd in utter disbelief.

George slumped over, and took his last breath. An immediate cloud fell over the household. Jeanette and everyone buckled into a depth of agonizing pain. Everyone was crying. Some were screaming. Jeanette's body positioned itself into contortion that seemed to have locked into this unusual position, and consoling her was not happening. She was in agony as we all were. George's life ended, so where does this leave Jeanette?

Jeanette will now have to live life without the love of her life. It could all be attributed to her insane jealousy. I could not believe that this was happening! Everybody knew that George's death was no accident, but he loved her so much, he did not want her to have to spend her life in prison. What a loving man!

We answered all the police questions, however, the questing soon concluded because George said it was an accident. We all gathered our belongings and headed to our homes.

Chapter 8

M A ANNA BEGAN TO UPDATE the group with as much as she knew about Mary. She received a letter from Trudy, Mary's niece in response to an inquiry to Mary's family members. I am sad to say that no one has heard from Mary. We can continue to pray for Mary and her family. This must be a trying time for all of them. I trust that when she is ready she will contact us. We miss her and we will always remember her for she was the inspiration for our gatherings.

We started out making a quilt for Mary, so many years ago. Her quilt was our first, and here we are many quilts and many years later with many quilts to our efforts, as God blesses many families through the executions of these fine ladies.

It amazes me how one day everything may be okay and the next day, things go awry. That is because our enemy is roaring after us. He may even attempt to and or delay the answers to our prayers, "The Bible" speaks about this in Daniel 10:13, as our antagonist works against us, however, we can rely upon God to see us through any challenging situation.

Mary was so sad about some disagreement that she had with Prince, and then with the report of his death just seem to push her over the edge.

All women are busy sewing as Ma Anna is speaking and at this rate, we may very well be starting the next quilt in a few days. Sappy is so excited at how quickly it is coming together.

I often picture Mary on the day of Prince's funeral, such a sad picture. It has been years and no one has heard from her. We know by now that she has left this town. We don't know where she traveled to, or where she is living or if she is living.

Well, may God bless her and keep her and maybe someday she will walk through that door, and show us the Mary that we knew. The last time we saw her, she was not the person that we knew. She had lost an incredible amount of weight, she was not talking. There was no laughter in her but just a sad and remorseful stranger among friends who love her.

We have to believe that whatever it is, wherever she is, she is unable to do any better then what she is doing. Our prayers remain with her.

May Dell, would you like to update us on the progress of your family?

"My pleasure," Ma Anna may Dell began. We are still a family in silence regarding our major problem. We seem not to know what to say or if to say and if we decide to say then we wrestle with how to say it, perhaps wrapping it in sugar so to speak. Maysee will sometimes show faint smiles when I make her a new dress when I style her hair. She never laughs out loud. As I think about it none of us laugh out loud. Our home is one of complete silence. I am through the help of you ladies, getting an opportunity to get years of bottled up anger, shame, disappointing things inside of me, off of my chest. I feel somewhat guilty for though it's late, I am still getting some relief, but what about Maysee? What about my other children, all of them have been teased, picked on and often in a very mean way. You know how cruel some children can be.

My husband, well that's a whole new story. He carries another kind of lonely silence one that he harbors solely as he struggles to make a living for his family. He too is silent for he can't even talk to me or me to him about this situation. I frequently think, what is he thinking, or if he is thinking about a situation that he can do nothing about. His workload is so heavy and so hard and demands so many of the hours in a day. When he comes home from a day's work of farming he is so worn down and so tired. He welcomes sleep, for it may be his only safe escape from a life that you cannot live in harmony with your family, there is no peace and neither can you escape. One must live on, and press on by the grace of God.

Chapter 9

SAPPY

THE GROUP CONVENED ON THE meeting day. Sappy can't wait to update everyone on her granddaughter and her Dad. She is eager to hear what these ladies think of the latest developments.

The Nurses in the facility where my dad is was laughing and having a good old time as they rushed to tell me what happened as my Dad was preparing to go to his class reunion. I could not wait to share this story. They were competing to be the one to assist him in dressing for his class reunion. So they could say "I dressed him" for his big day.

My Dad could not understand what all the fuss was about. He told the nurses about how Mom used to pick out his clothes, and how much she loved doing it.

They told me that he refused to wear a pink shirt, for he said his wife would never approve of him wearing a pink shirt. They offered him a wheelchair, to get him to the pickup point more quickly where he would be driven to his destination. He refused.

Why would he not ride in the wheelchair one of the ladies asked?

He is so proud. He holds onto his independence. We are amazed at how much he is still able to do. He is ninety-eight.

He said that his Daddy would turn over in his grave if he knew that he was being pushed in a wheelchair! He believes that we are a strong family and as long as we are able to maintain ourselves in an independent way we should do so. The nurses said he excused himself and left them standing there with the empty wheelchair and their mouths open as he strutted off saying "Excuse me, nurses, I am off to my family reunion." He intended to say class reunion.

The nurses were so afraid that he may have fallen, however, he did make it safely without falling, and altogether they breathe a sigh of relief.

I wished you could see the nurses showing me how his behaviors, his gestures, his attempts at still trying to strut as he did in his younger days. It was so funny.

Well as for my granddaughter, she graduated high school and she wanted to go to New York. She was offered two scholarships here, one at South Carolina State, and the other at Claflin University. I was so excited, I said she's going to college, but she wants to go somewhere else. She feels that the only thing she could do here was to become a teacher and teach school in the same school that she attended.

"What's wrong with that? Magnolia asked. It would be a great accomplishment.

Yes, it would be but I think she wants to see her Mom, her Mom lives up North, so she got it in her head that she wanted to do something different. You know when she was caring for her other grand mom, she told her that she was going to be a nurse and a good one and that prediction has stuck in her head. I believe that is the direction that her thinking is going. These young people change their minds from time to time.

"What is that scripture?" Ma Anna asked.

"Oh yes, I know. Bring up a child in the way he should go. That's it," Ma Anna confirmed. Leave her to God. Keep the prayers going for her, we all will pray for her as well and surely God will direct her path.

Anyway, she has found a job. She was so worried about getting a job. She tried for a job in a factory, and did not get it she was so disappointed. I assured her that God had a different plan for her life, and now she has a job. Her job is in a hospital. She helps the nurses, and she likes it very much. She is a Nurse's assistant. She has now expressed an interest in nursing school. That girl just loves to go to school, no matter what kind of school it is, but I want her to go to college.

Not to worry Sappy, she will get to college, providing that that is part of God's plan for her life. College is good, but not everybody has to go to college. Some students may not be able to go to college, or some may have other interests.

I believe, Ma Anna continued as we view our situation regarding our lack of knowledge. We may believe that only college can erase our so called lack of knowledge. But you see lack of knowledge is only a portion of our situation and or our present condition. We have had to have some knowledge, for we were knowledgeable enough to survive despite the harshest of circumstances.

The educational system did not include us, we were excluded. When it was said that we were included, the educational system was rigged heavily against us. The books were not the most current edition; pages were marred and or missing. We were kept out of school to work in the fields.

Despite all of these unequaled atrocities we continue to survive, thrive, and go on to the next grade level until we complete our studies. Somehow we stayed in the game, in the most unequal playing field.

Let us also encourage those who may not choose a college, but will do something positive with their life, and will positively contribute to the world. I believe when one of us achieve, we all achieve.

God wants his children to do well. We all do not have to learn to do our 'well' in a college, it could be college but it can also be in another arena. God will always be with us.

She still talks about this singer, now she knows his name. She talks about him nonstop and she is rearing to meet him. I have never seen anything like this in my entire life it is unbelievable.

Scripture time Ma Anna injected and all the women said in unison "Bring up a child in the way that she should go…" and they all joined in the laughter.

Sappy had to join in with their laughter. You women are constant reminders. Thank you for your reminders. You are all beginning to sound like Ma Anna.

That is a compliment Ma Anna said, for we are supposed to share conversations with younger generations so that they may keep the tradition going. We must sustain our families.

Well, my granddaughter reports that the nurses like her and she gets along well with them. But I tell you if that girl talks about that singer to her coworkers the way she talks about him to us, she will drive them away. When she gets on a topic she can wear you thin.

"She will be fine, Ma Anna said, she will be fine.

She has applied to become a licensed practical nurse. She is excited. The nurses are encouraging her. There is also a college component so if she gets accepted, I think we are soon to see our first in this family to attend college. The college component was added to set the stage for any student who may choose to go beyond the licensed practical nurse program. She probably will go further because that girl loves to go to school. She will be enrolling in September. After she completes the program, she will get a job in the hospital that she is currently working.

We are grateful; it is a blessing from God.

Chapter 10

MAGNOLIA

NOW LADIES REMEMBER, AS I shared information before about Louise, and the Kool-Aid she served to Grandma Cecelia? Louise was a large woman in statue and her size coupled with her mean spirit caused many to be intimidated by her. She seemed to like and or enjoyed the uneasiness that she bought to people, especially men. She enjoyed seeing them scrim.

As family members began talking about suspicions surrounding the death of her second husband, I began to remember from years long past when Will first told me about the rat poison in the Kool-Aid, and he was speaking just above a whisper. I believed that he was so afraid of Louise that he made a decision not to speak.

Louise scared his voice right out of him. She was married three times you know and the first husband's death was suspicious. I told you about the wine on the table after the social event, well that same night Louise was successful in coaxing others to prolong the party and come to her house. A few of the party-hardy group took her up on her offer. That is why she wanted the leftover bottles of wine from the tables, after the social gathering. She successfully convinced a few of the party hoppers to prolong the party.

Her husband was enjoying himself as were the others shortly after the group traveled to their home. They were dancing, drinking, laughing and seemed to be having fun. Her husband Henry said he felt tired and was going to lie down. Louise told him that he was not tired, we have guest. They are your guest Henry reminded her, you invited them I am tired now. They are our guest Louise corrected him, so you have to continue in our celebration. Celebrate as long as you wish Henry said, but I must lie down, I am too tired.

Louise grabbed him in the collar and backed him into their bedroom. She bellowed to the guest "Excuse us for a few minutes." The guest continued being engaged in drinking, laughing and dancing and having fun. The guest knew her and felt that it was not unusual for Louise to create drama whenever and wherever she congregated. This was a disagreement between husband and wife, nothing serious.

About five minutes after going into their bedroom Louise shouted Help! Help! Henry is not answering me. Henry was dead. That ended the party.

Everyone present thought Louise contributed to his death, perhaps not intentionally, but maybe accidentally because she was so rough. She wanted Henry to do what she wanted him to do and she did not allow him to have any say in the matter.

When he complained of feeling tired, perhaps he was becoming ill, who knows however he is now dead and we don't know how or why he died.

I heard another story about Louise and Henry, she was asking Henry something and Henry was involved with playing with his little nephew. The child was so gleeful Henry was caught up in playing with him.

"Did you hear me?" Louise asked, and she got no answer from Henry as he was playing with the child. Louise took a pail of scalding water and dash in Henry's direction and at that very moment the child was running to Jump on Henry's lap and she scaled Henry and the child it was such a cruel occurrence.

Anyway, everyone who was present was very suspicious of Louise because of her boisterous nature.

The women were surprised and, and remembered bits and pieces of this story but Louise was always the talk of the town. People were really afraid of her.

All the women said "Lord have mercy at the same time" as they prepared to adjourn.

Chapter 11

ELEANOR

Eleanor (left)

WELL, LADIES, IT IS NEEDLESS to say that the night that George died, it changed the life of everybody present that night, especially Jeanette. Every friend present was in dismal shock. We all kept asking, how could this happen? A party should be happy times and a joyous occasion turned out to be so sad, so dismal. And so excessively bloody!

As the police concluded their questioning—which turned out to be short, due to George's statement of it being an accident.

My sisters went on with their lives as all of us did, we had no choice—but now they disconnected totally from me. I now realized that George was the glue that held them somewhat close to me. I have not heard from my sisters or my mother since George's death.

I believe that my Mom cared for me in her own way, however, she loved my sisters in a different way from the way she loved me. I detected that she loved their father in a different way then she loved my father, and it showed in our interactions. It was apparent, or it was the way I felt, that she cared more for their father than she did for mine so she cared for them more than she cared for me. I may have been wrong, but wrong or right this is what I was feeling as a child, and nothing she did or said made me feel any different, from what I felt and those feelings bore deeply into my being. But whatever love I received from whomever, I receive it and am grateful to God for it.

This, I believe is one of the ways that God is making things work together for my good.

As of now, I am forever grateful to God that I have a loving husband, and my children feel the love that my husband and I have for them. I cannot make someone love me. God loves me and he has given me a family, and we love each other unconditionally. If I had not experienced this lack of love from my sisters and mother, I would never have been able to feel so much appreciation of a loving family. This, I believe is one of the ways that God is making things work together for my Good.

It has taught me to love my children deeply and make them feel the love that I have for them. I want them to know how special they are each of them to me and they know their Mother and Father love them, without a doubt.

We think of My Mom and my sisters often, and we wonder how they are doing, but we can't understand how families can drift so far apart like this. I know my mother will never know my children as she may know my sister's children, I don't even know if either of my sisters have children. My children know and love the grandmother on their Father's side but there is very little I can say about my Mother to them. I tell them that she moved away and I am not sure where they live now because the last letters that were mailed to them were returned to me, with no forwarding address.

They moved away to another state, I don't know where. I was hurt, yes for after all we are sisters I had not shared that with anyone, for I am sure that I had not realized the weight of this that I was carrying until now, for I feel so much lighter, and I thank you ladies from the bottom of my heart for listening to me and share my burden. You know we all are affected differently by our circumstances, and this proves to me that my burden was even heavier than I realized but thank God we are here to help and uplift each other that is what I believe that God had in mind when he said to love one another.

I appreciate the love and prayers that you all have shared with me. Eleanor gently embraced the woman sitting closest to her and drifted into soft sniffles as she quoted the scripture" My God shall supply all my needs according to his riches in glory, Thank you, Jesus.

The other woman echoed her, "Thank you, Jesus!!"

Chapter 12

MAY DELL

M A ANNA REPORTS THAT SHE received a correspondence
from Trudy, Mary's niece–however, she still has not heard
from Mary. Trudy and her family are well and she sends well
wishes to all of us. She now lives in Stamford, Conn. and she likes
Connecticut very much. She plans to visit as soon as she is able to.
She communicates with the remainder of her family and neither of
them has heard from her aunt Mary.

Ma Anna than asked May Dell if she would like to update the group as to the state of her family. And whatever concerns they may be experiencing.

Well, May Dell began, Maysee finished high school and she has her mind now set on getting married. School was such a painful experience for her; I can imagine that she will not even consider continuing her education. I wish she would not focus upon getting married, however, I believe that she just need to escape this house of silence, and also the school environment. Therefore, I don't believe that she will even consider going to college. She probably fears that she may experience the same treatment that she received in high school, she can't think beyond those times.

I asked her if she was absolutely sure that marriage is what she wants to do, she says yes. I think she really believes it, but I pray that she will change her mind.

In life we may ask ourselves that question, and our answer to self maybe yes I am sure, but how can we be absolutely sure? Even when we think that we are sure, as our life unfolds things may change. We can be sure one minute one day and the very next day we may not be as sure.

Maysee went on to marry a young man from the Dunson Family who lived in the next county. They seemed to be a nice family. Maysee became more talkative. Her demeanor changed. I began to hear her laugh she expressed more happiness then I had ever seen before. I was pleased that she was having some fun.

Unfortunately, after about three months, she seemed to have dropped back into silence. She stopped laughing aloud. I was curious as to what may have happened. I questioned her; however, she assured me that things were fine. I knew something was different, however, I thought only that the honeymoon phase of this marriage had just ended and Maysee is now delving into her housewife routines.

A mother knows her children, we notice changes, we pick up on those changes no matter how sullen, and or blatant, we see changes, especially negative changes, and this felt like a negative change.

The harder children try to conceal, the more the thing they want to contain, is revealed proportionately to the depth of the desire to keep it concealed.

I observed a black and blue mark on her neck. It was covered partly by her sweater. My antennas went up sharply. That told me that her new husband may be abusive. He displayed such a kind and gentleman demeanor, polite, I did not want to jump to conclusions however how else would she experience a black and blue mark on her neck?

We later learned that he was abusive, and her very light skin revealed the results of the more frequent episodes of abuse. She tried to deny, conceal and not involve her family; however, that kind of shame makes it worse for the victim. She did not want to involve her brothers, for anything might happen when brothers try to protect sisters.

I told her brothers and they had a confrontation, and for a while, there were no marks, as we could see and Maysee said that things were alright. We visited more frequently, sending the message to her husband that Maysee family was very concerned about her, and would do whatever they needed to do to protect her.

About two months later after our last visit, it was obvious that he abused her and she displayed many marks of abuse. Word spread around that Maysee's husband was abusive to her. The old Massa heard about it. Old Massa is aged now, I am unsure of how he heard about the abuse Dunson was inflicting upon Maysee. The bold Massa went to Maysee's home and though he had never uttered a word prior to this day as to being Maysee's father, he marched right into Maysee's and Dunson's home, and walked up to Dunson's face, while pointing his long white finger between Dunson's eyes and told him.

"If you put your hands on my child again, that will be the last time you raise your hands! Believe me!" and he marched right out of the house. The nerve of that Massa.

After the Massa's family heard about the Massa going to the Dunsons, they did not know what Massa said to them. Only the Dunsons experienced what transpired. Massa family explained that the Massa was having some memory problems and asked the Dunsons to disregard anything he may have said, for he does not know what he is saying.

The Negros felt that he knew exactly what he was saying and felt that, that may have been the at least one truth that he told. The boldness, even at his age, he had no fear of going into a Negro home regardless of the reason.

Once again a difference in opinions.

That was the day that Maysee learned the reason why she looked so different from her siblings. I wish it did not happen this way but it did and I can't change it. I ask God to forgive me for not being able to find the words to talk about this with Maysee. The words never came.

Dunson must have believed Massa. He could not stop when the brothers asked him to, he could not stop even when they beat him to a pulp, but when the white man told him he would never raise his hand again, he believed him, He stopped. I wonder why?

I grieve for my child. It seems that sadness follows her everywhere she goes. We want the best for our children, I am not promoting separations, yet when one is abused one must protect self from that environment.

That is not the way that God intended that married life should be. Husbands are ordered by the Lord to love your wife! He should love her as Christ loved the church. Abuse is clearly not an expression of love.

The sadness of this situation grabbed the group. They offered prayer and support that Maysee and her family would be protected, and that their lives would move forward in a more positive way.

The group prayed silently, sending up individual prayers for May Dell and Maysee's families, knowing that God was in their midst.

They quietly prepared for closure and their journeys back to their homes.

Chapter 13

MAGNOLIA

I WANT TO CONTINUE TELLING YOU all about Louise and her husband, Magnolia said. Today I am going to tell you about Louise's husband number two. He too was a bit boisterous, more boisterous than her husband number one. Everybody was saying that Louise got her match in husband number two. His behavior was similar to hers. They both had their own personal pistols. I guess they did not trust each other.

Late one afternoon, they brawled with each other, which is their normal. They were rolling all over the floor. They each must have gotten the idea at the same time, to grab their weapons. They jumped and ran for their pistols. Well, they ran as much as they each could run for they were both large people. Each pulled their pistols, not only did they pulled their pistols. They both pulled the trigger and in an attempt to shoot each other it resulted in both of them hitting the floor at the same time. They both laid still, each thinking that they had shot the other.

Lo' and behold, it became very quiet, contrasted with the noise that was present, prior to the sound of the shots from each of the pistols, but immediately after the pistols were fired the house went quiet. And they both lay still on the floor.

They lived to tell the story of how each thought the other was hit by the bullet. They were both fearful to move. They both lay still for no one knows how long. A nosey neighbor came over and discovered them lying on the floor as he could see them by peering through the screened door. He rushed inside as he too thought they were dead as he could see blood on the floor. They both were bleeding.

The good neighbor got the husband to sit up and as he sat up he saw the blood and fainted, and Louise followed suit, she stirred and saw the blood and she also fainted.

The good neighbor got the doctor who did make house calls. They both had to be admitted into the county hospital. They healed, came home and picked up right where they left off started with catfights and ended up in bear struggles over minor issues.

Not long after they shot each other he died. No one believed he died of natural causes. The neighbors thought she killed him. No one knows how or why, neither did anyone cared. There was no investigation, it was just accepted that he died of natural causes.

It seemed that the entire neighborhood breathed a sigh of relief, for they all were sick and tired of hearing stories of Louise and Pete, or Pete and Louise. The police were tired of calls from the neighborhood.

You know some women have a gift for turning on the honey until the beau is trapped, in this case, until the bear is trapped. Bears like honey also, and this bear was trapped. When trappings are in play, more often than not, a life is lost. This case was no different. I believe there is a name for people who like to fight all the time.

We can't start out wrong and end up right.

Something is wrong if you are always in disharmony. That is certainly not the life that God wants for his servants. I guess that was the problem, Louise was not a servant, for if she was she would not, and could not do some of the things that she did. It may be confusing as we are not able to earn our way, for we should be dependent upon God for he is our provider. However, we should strive to choose the right thing to do in any circumstance. That is why we have to choose the right thing to do from the beginning. We can't start out wrong and end up right, that is surely a no-win situation.

Well, you know that God wants us to serve each other, and fighting and attempting to hurt each other is not serving each other. The service that we render to each other should be service as unto the Lord. So this fighting and disharmony is not the service that God instructs us to render as unto him.

He said what so ever things are good, what so ever, you know the scripture; think on these things (Philippians 4:8)

Chapter 14

INSTANT CHANGE

Anna   John

NOTHING SHOCKED THE PATCHWORK ORGANIZATION more than the death of Papa John. He was up and about fulfilling his usual activities and had a stroke. From which he never recovered. The Doctor visited him at his home, there was no hospital. He lingered a few days but more than likely he had another stroke and died.

It shook Ma Anna to her core, however, because she was such a God-fearing woman she was able to deal with her most painful loss. He was indeed the light of her world, her bouncing pad, her mailman, and the love of her life. He was full of whimsical laughter, and his laughter was always in the air. His laughter was catching, as you heard him laughing, soon you will be laughing also.

Just three months after she lost Papa John, Grandma Carrie's husband died. His death was due to a heart attack. Grandma Carrie's children came and took her to live with them in New York City and, this became yet another shock and readjustment for the organization.

Ma Anna's primary consultant was now in a faraway state; however, they did continue to communicate by mail.

At this point the Patchwork organization has been operating for over four decades. It has touched the lives of many families, and has contributed to warmth and teachings to the participants and their families.

Ma Anna continued the business of Patchwork until the introduction of comforters. Comforters came into existence approximately around 1956.

The comforter was a warm and lighter bed covering that families became interested in. The comforter provided warmth; however, it could not provide the love, the prayers, and the concern that was shared by each of the families as they sang, as they sewed, as they prayed. Those loved ones were being covered by the love of God as his love and care had been infused into the covering for every family who received them.

There is no way that bed coverings manufactured by a machine could deliver the humane part of the love infusion that was so much a part of the homemade bed coverings. That is why prayer was such a part of the meetings. Those prayers went with the coverings. That is why the stories were shared. To help the families to stop any negativity that had taken up a place in that family.

Also, there came to be a new wave of women joining the workforce and even competing with the men to hold the same kind of jobs as the men. The women felt that there was no need to make quilts, they had so-called 'better jobs' to reach for, not thinking about how important it is to maintain a strong family unit.

Our immediate families were assigned to us by God to help teach us how to mingle with our larger family in the world. If you are fighting with your immediate family, then you can expect to fight with your larger family.

There is a reason that God put that family member in your family and there is a reason he brings the person from the larger world across your path.

There came to be very few women who wanted to make quilts. Families than became determined to buy this new bed covering so the organization continued to diminish.

In 1959 Ma Anna died as a result of a stroke. The physical organization died with her. The younger women relished her memory and all the teachings she shared, however, they had very little desire to make quilts. Trudy, Mary's niece was the most knowledgeable younger woman who had an interest in the women who were partakers of the patchwork organization.

Trudy traveled back and forth to South Carolina to attend each of the funerals. Upon each trip, she gathered whatever information she could to share with others. She felt very indebted to the group and felt that in memory of Ma Anna and Papa John, Grandma Carrie and the group from the Patchwork quilting circle. Trudy wanted to connect, with families who were involved in any way by the Patchwork seamstresses and teachers. She planned to somehow attempt at putting closure on this group. It gave her something to hold on to since it seemed that she had lost complete contact with her beloved Aunt Mary who was really her second Mother this would make her feel good and it would be like a loving memory to Aunt Mary.

Each letter Trudy received, each trip she was able to gather bits and pieces of information, she cherished, each letter each bit of information about as many members as she could to ensure that this group would never be forgotten, as they were foundational in their core purpose which was to teach and encourage others to share information between generations. We are to be about building. Every generation should not be about building foundations, we should be building upon the foundation from the previous generation.

We must close the gap between generations. We need to find a way to bridge the gap and avoid allowing the gap to broaden; we must listen to each other. The elders must respect the mind of the youth, and not feel that age give them carte blanche to wisdom. Many of the aged are not wise.

If we live we will age however, wisdom does not come automatically. If we are receptive to wisdom, we need God's help to get it. God said if you lack wisdom to ask for it. Why would God waste his wisdom on someone who will not use it? He invites us to ask, he may feel if you ask then you will be willing to use your wisdom to help the world.

James 1:5 "If any of you lack wisdom, let him ask of God, that giveth to all men liberally, and unbraideth not; and it shall be given him."

Elders how can you say that a younger person has not ask God for wisdom? They may be the avenue that God has chosen to bring information to you. Be open to receive, to share, despite the changes that we see in the world we must continue to connect, generation to generation.

Chapter 15

BITS AND PIECES

Trudy (Right)

I, TRUDY HAVE, AND WILL continue to gather and share bits and pieces about all the women that were involved in the Patchwork organization. I will share the bits and pieces as I gathered information about the group. As of now, this is what has transpired;

My beloved Aunt Mary has disappeared no one has heard from her. Sometimes I feel as if she has disappeared from the face of the earth.

Sappy's granddaughter did make it to college; she was the first in her family. She graduated from nursing school, went on to college and graduated. And pursued Health care education. Her grandfather was blessed to witness that family milestone before he passed on.

The male singer's name that she waited by the radio to hear was Brook Benton. The song he sang was "It's Just A Matter of Time".

Magnolia's family member Louise went on to marry yet a third husband. He had epilepsy and was taking a medication called Dilantin.

He became deathly ill and the doctors could not figure out why he was becoming more ill and his seizures were occurring more frequently. The doctors requested that he bring his medicines in and when he did the doctors noticed that some of the capsules of Dilantin had been tampered with.

The lab analysis reported the drug Dilantin had been removed from the capsules and replaced with rat poison. Louise was arrested for tampering with a drug with the intention of aggregation and possibly for attempted murder as a result of drug tampering. I was not clear on all charges, but I know she is in prison.

Magnolia's family, her Mom and her sisters Jeanette and Andrea her sisters moved away and was not heard from again. She misses them but is contented with her current loving family.

May Dell's daughter Maysee moved away. We heard that she left Dunson, shortly after the night Massa stormed into her home. It was said that she moved to Paris and was 'passing' in her new location. Many youngsters who were off springs of white and black couples if their skin was white enough; they would choose to pass for white in an effort to be treated better.

Maysee may have been assisted by her Massa Father, in her escape from her abusive husband.

This concludes all my bits and pieces at this time.

Chapter 16

REFLECTIONS BY TRUDY

D URING THE PERIOD OF THE Patchwork era in the State
of South Carolina, there was great tension among the races.
They did not mix If they did no one would know, it was kept secret.
These were the times when white children rode school buses and
Negro children as they walked many miles to school; they were
often run off of the road by the adult white bus drivers. The sparsely
filled school buses of white children laughed gleefully as the
Negro children tried to scramble to safety, as they felt the cascade
of spitballs, rocks, pecans, old books or anything that the white
children had in their possession, and felt delighted in throwing in
the Negro children's direction.

The bus driver would slow down and or stop the bus momentarily,
to allow the white children to experience what they felt was fun.

I was seven years old at the beginning of this story, today I am
forty seven. I am remembering my Aunt Mary and how she and I
cried for days as I reflect on when Prince went off to the army. We
knew that our lives would be so different without him.

It was a very cruel and divided South during these times. I have to take you back to the distant past when this began. It was my early days of living with Aunt Mary. I begin by sharing a conversation between Aunt Mary and I.

"It's about time you come inside Trudy" Aunt Mary called out to me.

"Oh, please Aunt Mary" I begged. I'd like to stay out just a bit longer so I can see the lighting bugs, just a little while longer, please?

"It's getting dark Trudy." "I'd like to get to bed early, I want you inside soon." Aunt Mary responded.

It's ok Aunt Mary go to sleep, I promise I will come in right after I see the lightning bugs. I would like to catch one. How do they make light? Their tails just light up like flashlights.

I was chasing a lightning bug when I saw someone walking in my direction.

"Hello Trudy," said a deep voice that I recognized as he ran to meet me.

Prince! Prince! I shouted happily.

Sssshhh sssshhhh, he cautioned I'd like to surprise Mary we can play together for a little while. Then I will go and see your Aunt Mary.

"My, how you have grown, and in such a short while. I have been in the army for six months and you did all that growing in six months? Wow!"

"My Prince! That's what I called him I was so happy to see him! Aunt Mary will be happy to see him too!

Prince was a serious man, yet he was playful. He was firm but kind. He stood six feet three inches. His beautiful brown skin would glisten when there was sunlight. He had an intensity that was piercing. His silence was hard for some to endure. When he spoke, he got attention.

Prince and Aunt Mary adored each other. She was happiest when Prince came to visit. He was the light of her world, and he and I were the best of friends. Aunt Mary and I never could imagine that Prince would not be in our life.

Aunt Mary and I cried for days when Prince went off to the army. And I am still crying periodically about his death, as I look back on the beautiful time I spent with him, we played hopscotch until the dusk, and we caught lightning bugs, I have such beautiful memories of him. He was so obliging to the people he loved. We knew that our lives would be so different without him. After my Mom and Dad were both killed in that awful car accident, I came to live with Aunt Mary. She was going to marry Prince one day. I just knew it!

With Prince's help, I caught my lightning bug and reluctantly came inside, for I promised Aunt Mary I would come inside. Prince and I skipped to the wing of the house to my bedroom. Boy, this house is big!

"I remembered how you begged Mary for your room. I forgot how far away from her room that was. You each have your wing."

Yes, Aunt Mary did not want to give it to me but I convinced her that I was a big girl, soon to be eight years old and it was okay.

I hurriedly prepared myself for the bed for I knew that Prince would read me a bedtime story if I hurried.

"Once upon a time" Prince began. "There were three little bugs who wanted to have a meeting to talk about their friendship. It was a ladybug, a beetle bug, and a lightning bug." We laughed. Before he could get far into the story, I was falling asleep. "We'll continue another time," he said, go to sleep.

"Good night my Prince, I said groggily, "Good night my Trudy, I will tell Mary I tucked you in, and she might be asleep by now."

Prince tiptoed toward the long corridor that would take him to the other end of the large home. I snuggled deep into the covers and slipped deeper into sleep.

I could not wait to see Aunt Mary the next morning. I wanted to talk about Prince. "Guess who I saw last night?" I asked.

"Who did you see? Aunt Mary inquired looking puzzled.

I saw Prince.

"You saw Prince?" Aunt Mary asked. Looking even more puzzled.

"Yes I saw him, He came to see me. Did you think he was going to see you, and not see me? I saw him first." I teased Aunt Mary. "After all, he is my Prince too."

"Didn't he tell you that he tucked me in? He tried to read me a bedtime story but I was too sleepy after chasing those lighting bugs. Prince helped catch one I still have him in a jar Prince put holes in the lid of the jar so the lighting bugs could have air, Aunt Mary I...."

"Trudy please stop already!" Aunt Mary interrupted me abruptly.

"What is the matter, Aunt Mary?" I asked.

Aunt Mary did not answer but she was not her usual self after seeing Prince. She was behaving very different. She appeared nervous and tensed. She said she was happy to see Prince however there was something different. She implied that they had a big disagreement and she was not sure if he would ever come back again.

"He'll be back Aunt Mary I tried to assure her. He has to come back."

"I am not sure he will," Aunt Mary said;

"Well I am sure," I said to her. "He will come back to see us."

"Trudy, no more talk about Prince please, we must go on."

"What did you disagree about?" She did not reply, she just appeared very sad.

About a month later Prince's uncle visited Aunt Mary and asked her had she seen Prince. Aunt Mary informed him that she did not expect to hear from Prince, as they had a big disagreement the last time Prince paid her a visit.

The uncle then disclosed that he was worried that Prince was due to come home about a month ago, on leave, and he did not come. That is not like Prince.

The uncle informed Aunt Mary that their family received a letter from the United States Army saying he was away without official leave.

Mary was surprised to hear him say that Prince did not come home. She knew she saw him exactly a month prior, She remembers that he came late evening, we disagreed, and when he left I was sure he went home to his family. She had not seen him since, and she assumed he went on to visit his family and then back to the army.

"We did not see him." his uncle responded.

"You did not see him?" Mary repeated.

"We did not see him" Uncle responded.

"Oh God, Oh God" Mary moaned. "Has something happened to him?" She questioned.

"Why do you think that?" uncle inquired...?

"I feel that way because of what we talked about when we last met."

"Tell me?" Uncle asked.

"I can't uncle." Mary responded, "But I know he was here about a month ago and I have not seen or heard from him since that day."

"Let me head back so I can let the family know. I think we must file a missing person's report."

"Please let me know if you hear anything at all and certainly I will do the same."

"I sure will uncle responded, I sure will. I am so sorry you had a disagreement, but not to worry that it can be fixed. Take care of yourself." He waved goodbye as he rode off on his bicycle.

Prince's family filed a missing person's report with the police department and began the wave of waiting and hoping for the best.

Some time later a body was hauled from the old Santee River outside of the district of his home town, thereby rendering the investigation to the next town. The body was spotted by fishermen. It had ropes and tapes attached which would suggest that it was tied to something. Not far from the resurgence of the body an old car motor was obtained by divers with pieces of rope matching the rope that was attached to the remainder of the body.

Investigations showed that the body was tied to an old car motor for the purpose of holding it down into the depths of that old river, but it emerged and made itself visible.

The body was identified and confirmed as that of Prince though the dog tag that with the body and further by army dental records. Once again and finally, Prince displayed his presence in death as he so often did in life. His quiet presence was always known. There was a short investigation and too soon the case was filed with cases to be further investigated.

There was a short investigation and this time the case was filed with records of unsolved mysteries.

TRUDY'S FAMILY REUNION

MANY FAMILIES ARE RETURNING TO their home towns to attend a family reunion. It's been over forty years! I am aboard a touring bus that drives the families throughout the old homestead.

I was raised mostly, by my aunt Mary; however I have close ties with all of my aunts from both Mom and Dad sides of my families. I would not miss this for the world! I look forward to seeing all my family members, but I am sad that Aunt Mary won't be there for no one was able to contact her for no one knows how to get in touch with her.

I can't wait to see the old house where Ma Anna held her Patchwork meetings. As the bus slowly passes through the old homestead the members are interacting and exchanging memories of days gone by.

One story is shared, to demonstrate to the youth aboard what real love is all about. It was the love story of Minnie and Ralph. Ralph walked from one town to the next, which was quite a distance, during their courtship. The bus is approaching Minnie's old home, it still stands. Ralph was so relieved when Minnie said yes to his proposal for those walks were taking a toll on him. The walks and also the piercing looks and detailed questioning from Minnie's father.

I then began to talk about the areas that we were passing as much as I could remember from my past, and what was shared with me.

Suddenly the bus driver informs the group that there is a boy, riding a bicycle riding furiously, behind the bus and he is waving a piece of paper. I think he wants us to stop. It seems he is trying to get our attention. Let's stop to see what he wants. The driver slows down and the boy catches up and is riding along side of the bus and the driver stops, the boy enters the bus. Everyone is quietly waiting to hear what the boy has to say.

"Good afternoon everyone, my name is Louis, is there someone on this bus named Trudy?"

"Yes, I am Trudy," I answered him.

"How do I know that you are Trudy?"

"Well, I know that I am Trudy. I tell you, I am Trudy."

"Do you like lightning bugs?" the boy asked?

I immediately thought of Aunt Mary and the evening that Prince came to see us. Only she and Prince knew how much I liked lightning bugs.

"Yes, I like lightning bugs doesn't everyone?"

"Ms. Mary told me that this letter is for Trudy's eyes only."

"I am Trudy please give me the letter as I anxiously scrambled to snatch it from his hands, so I could open it, did you say, Ms. Mary?"

"Yes mam, Ms. Mary," he replied.

"But my Aunt Mary disappeared from here right after Prince's funeral and no one has heard from her it has been over forty years. Her family does not know where she is."

"She came here yesterday."

Everyone is as surprised as I am as I opened the unevenly scribbled print and I read silently:

Dear Trudy,

Please come to see me. You must come alone. I am very old. Forgive me for being out of touch. I am very old, and I don't know how many years, months' weeks, days and or hours that I may have left.

It was all I could do to get here. But I prayed to God as Ma Anna and Grandma Carrie taught us to pray, I prayed and God spared me. I need to speak with you. I beg you to come. The boy will bring you to me.

Aunt Mary

I shared with family, it is from Aunt Mary!

"Mary, Mary" the older family members echoed.

"I have to go to her, but she wants me to come alone. I have to honor her wishes I will update you when I return."

"Karen, please talk to family in my absence."

"Ok," Karen said. "Continue the tour as planned."

"Is it far from here?" I asked the boy.

"Just over that hill" the boy, pointed.

"I'll drive you back there the bus driver." said he turned to go in the opposite direction. The boy biked in front of the bus, the driver followed, as the boy led the way. The boy stopped in front of a very large old house. The grass and shrubbery had grown so much around the house I hardly recognized it. I followed the boy into the shabby unkempt dwelling as we walked past unkempt shrubbery but I followed an abbreviated path that led to the steps that would take you inside. As we entered a room, in the far corner from a distance, her back was facing me and I observed a small frail frame and heard a voice which neither frame nor voice appeared to be of any resemblance to my Aunt Mary.

"Aunt Mary is that you I called out?"

"Trudy is that really you a raspy voice so low I could barely hear it speak."

"Please don't look at me," she asked. I began to silently question myself.

All kinds of crazy thoughts rushed through my head. Could this be my aunt Mary, or is this someone who may be an imposter, who perhaps heard about our family reunion, and knows our story.

"Is it really you?" I asked her again.

"It is what's left of me I have something that I must tell you." She took considerable time as she said each sentence.

"Please don't come any closer and don't ask any questions just let me try to get through telling you what I have to say. I can finally get this load up off of me."

It was hard but I stayed in my tracts as I inched closer. I tried to anticipate what she wanted to tell me.

"Trudy" she finally began again.

"For the last forty years I have carried this and it's about time that I lay this burden down. I ran away from this place years ago, never intending to return, ever, but for the last forty years no matter where I have been in the world, I would always awaken in this very room, every night of my life."

She seemed to gain strength as she continued to speak.

"Do you remember the night when Prince came here from the army?"

"Yes, mam I certainly do that was the last time we saw our beloved Prince alive."

"Well do you remember the chief of police Eugene Sword?"

"Yes, mam."

"Oh lord it hurts me so deeply to tell you this but I must. Trudy Gene Sword would pick certain Negro women that he wanted to be with and he would be with them. Whoever he wanted to, as often as he wanted to. Even if they had boyfriends and or a husband. He especially targeted women who had boyfriends in the service, for he knew the man would be away fulfilling his service to the country. If he chooses a woman who had a husband and or boyfriend who was not in the service, he would arrange for his deputy to pick up the man for some trumped-up charge and hold him in the police station after accusing him of some non-sense crime and question him for whatever length of time that was necessary as to avoid being surprised by the man's sudden appearance.

When his sexual encounter was over he would request to be picked up and when he got back to the station, the man would be released.

The women were threatened that if they did not cooperate, something dreadful would happen to their boyfriend and or their husband. The women were so afraid for their husbands, they would not dare breathe a word, for they knew that the husbands or boyfriends could be hurt badly or even killed and nothing would be done about it.

I let out a big gasp of disbelief at what Aunt Mary was telling me and stepped closer to Aunt Mary.

Trudy, please don't come any closer or I may not be able to finish this. I need to finish, God knows I need to finish. The longer she talked, the stronger the sounds, as if she was getting some instant relief.

I stopped again, just arm distance from her now but I made a sincere effort to respect her wishes.

With tears in her voice, she continues "this is the bad part, Gene sword was in my room that night"

"What!?' I gasp again.

"The chief of police?"

"The Chief of Police. Prince intended to surprise me that night, however, as he tiptoed into my room, at first, I thought it was you but it was dark; I would have gotten up and walked you back to your wing. It was Prince. He reached in the dark and tried to touch my head, instead, he touched the head of Gene Sword. Both men were surprised, and a scuffle ensued and Gene Sword grabbed his clothes as best he could and got out of the house. It happened so quickly and in the dark. I was stunned, and so was Prince.

We sat in silence for a long time. When Prince finally found his voice he questioned.

"You are my girl how could this happen,"

"I had no choice, I cried out to him. "I am so sorry you found out this way, but I was afraid to tell you. I have been taken over and over again. I am so sorry."

He frequently reminded me that he was on police business and if it became anything other than that the man would have to pay the penalty. He made that threat in some form each time he came. I was caught up in a relationship that I had not chosen, and I felt there was no way out.

"Why didn't you tell me?" Prince asked, then he stormed out of my house before I could answer, and I sat in a chair for the remaining of the night, angry, distraught and, not knowing what to do. That's why it was painful to talk to you the next morning about Prince, for I did not know what to think, or what to do, and I could not talk to anyone.

Chapter 18

THERE IS MORE

T RUDY STAY THERE, THERE IS still more to tell, bear with me I am almost done, if you embrace me I won't be able to finish please let me finish.

I am in such shock! I can hardly move yet I have to go to her. I care so much for my long lost aunt, I am shaking! She and I have been separated for so long until I might hurt her if I embrace her, for she looks so frail. I am still a small distance from her, as I hang on to her every word. Then she begins again.

"Gene Sword's wife sent for me I am not sure how she found me, his family begged me to come for they said he was screaming, Mary Sultry, please get Mary Sultry in his confusion. The wife and daughter took care of my expenses. They could not explain why it was so important for him to see me but I felt he was becoming confused.

I was skeptical about coming; however, I remembered all the prayers and lessons that Ma Anna and Grandma Carrie and the women in the Patchwork organization shared, so I came. They had been searching for me for months; they had the use of the police inquiries to look for my whereabouts. It was they who told me about our family reunion, and I felt that this was probably an indication that I needed to come back, so I decided to come.

The wife stated she felt her husband was close to death and she would appreciate that he might die more peaceful if I came.

When I arrived his wife went in to tell him I arrived, she came back and walked me into his bedroom and I sat. She left me momentarily with him and I was not prepared for what he said in a raspy deathlike voice "pl–pl-ease for-give me, I kill-ed Prince."

"I screamed."

The wife and daughter quickly ran back into the room, asking me what's wrong, what's wrong?

All I could do was point at him, as he took his last breath, they did not know what he said to me, and I did not share it with them, for what purpose would it have served?

A colored woman could not accuse a white man of Ralep, in the state of South Carolina during those days or any other state for that matter.

Raelp I asked, what's Ralep still standing a small distance from Aunt Mary.

It was a way, it was a way—she began to stammer as the pain from the memory engulfs her. "It was a word that the women created and shared as they tried to ask for help, but had no one to get help. It was a way that they let each other know that they were experiencing the same pain, the same disrespect, the shame, and of course the same fear. When they found courage enough to speak quietly to each other regarding their predicament.

Aunt Mary began rocking back and forth as if the rocking and the telling someone were bringing some closure.

Some of those men were very mean and sometimes that word ralep, (a combination of the word rape and help) was the last word for some of the women, who may have been beaten or maybe even killed.

I bolted to Aunt Mary. I could not contain myself. I am crying intensely! Neither of us was able to console the other. We held each other as both of our bodies shook ever so vigorously, releasing what was forty years of pent up love, hate, anger, pain, and grief.

The tears exploded forward like a burst of rain from both of us. It was a tear flood as we expelled the cleansing fluid of tears that continued to flow from each of us. The tears were so many; they actually formed a pool of water as they ran together. They flowed in the same direction, and joined together and floated down the few stairs and ran into the Santee River joining the body of water where Prince's body once laid.

We cried for what felt like hours, each of us feeling as if the other would never stop. We both was clutched in an unbreakable embrace, that served as the beginning of an old eraser for the years of absence, that perhaps will begin the healing process of our absence from each other.

We finally got to know what happened to Prince. We needed to bring closure, for the death of a man who touched both our lives in such a profound way, by his presence and now again by his absence.

We finally broke our embrace, and both chided in Unisom "Rest in peace, our beloved Prince."

Aunt Mary and I stayed for the remainder of the day and continued throughout the night reminiscing and finally able to look intently at each other.

Aunt Mary burst into song:

"Burdens down lord, Burdens down, lord I finally laid my burden down. I feel better, so much better since I laid my burden down."

Aunt Mary was not ready to see the family just yet. She and I will join the bus tour the next day. Aunt Mary will be traveling back to Stamford Connecticut with me, and the two of us will not be separated again.

When we get to Connecticut, in an effort to contribute to the next generation, we will start a gathering, where we can interact and share stories. We won't be making quilts but we can continue to do patchwork as Ma Anna and Grandma Carrie did Yes we can Aunt Mary echoed, yes we can!

"But they that wait upon the lord shall renew their strength; they shall mount up like eagles; they shall run and not be weary and they shall walk and not faint" (KJV)

Magnolia (left)   Carrie
Andrea (right)

George   Jeanette

Louise

Maysee

Prince

CPSIA information can be obtained
at www.ICGtesting.com
Printed in the USA
BVHW032149221020
591670BV00011B/63

9 781951 775421